KEEP

Also by Deborah Poe:

Hélène (Furniture Press)

the last will be stone, too
(Stockport Flats Press, Limited Edition)

Elements (Stockport Flats Press)

Our Parenthetical Ontology (CustomWords)

KEEP

Deborah Poe

DUSIE

Grateful acknowledgement is made to the editors of the journals in which pieces of this book first appeared: *Handsome, above/ground press, Dusie Press Tuesday Project, Turntable & Blue Light, eccolinguistics, Solid Quarter, Coconut, Court Green, Horseless Review #17, Posit, Loose Change, Touch the Donkey.*

Cover image: *What and Where*, Greg Dunn

Layout and design by DUSIE

Deborah Poe, first printing, 2018.

Author photo: Matthew Meisel

ISBN-13: 978-1-944253-07-3
LCCN: 2018957821

KEEP

I am another yourself   13

CARTOGRAPHY

The Sensual Infrastructure   19
Encode   21
Storage   22
Retrieval   23
Keep   24
Through the lens of memory, to collect for the next   25
Place is not a vessel   26

COORDINATES

Lacuna   31
Long ago dreaming   32
Memory of combat   33
Wild Kingdom   34
Paris   35
My funny Valentine   36
Taos   37
Interplace   38
Bellingham (The Butch Sunrise Mix)   42
Breath   43
Letter to B   44

SIGNS

you're the sister's boyfriend   49
holographic   50
spices lend from   51
a tiny car and   52
nuclear explosion   53
the pulling in   54
in laughing class   55
wake with panic open string   56
there was no day before it was a dream   57
even though you can fly   58
Travis' smell outside the rear window   59
a highly intricate book   60
how a poem fits into the day   61

PROUNS

a mansion made of stone binds to self   67
proun   68
proun   70
proun   72
proun   74
proun   76
proun   78
proun   80

NOTES   82

I AM ANOTHER YOURSELF

the cliffs cut between two countries
displace agitation between two hemispheres
such mountainous territories of mind

there is luxury to write this
(the baking, the sleeping, the shooting)
by the time you've read this, quadrillions of signals fire

there's no soul, no twenty one grams
what's left? brain, two percent of the body's weight,
seizes a chunk of the body's oxygen and bolts

at a museum, the Ferrari's plaque
reads aluminum and titanium
not watercolor, acrylic, or oil

the nervous system trajects information
like heart circulates your blood
nerves, bone, and steel—objects we have in common

below the bridge (which could always be blown up)—
in the last few seconds what you and I remember
relies on synapses, mental acts, artifacts

fresh tortillas, front yard, the writing on the wall.

cartography

*Let us try putting memory back into the lived world, where it has always
been in any event.*
    Edward S. Casey, *Descriptions*

*Of course, the brain is a machine and a computer—everything in classical
neurology is correct. But our mental processes, which constitute our being
and life, are not just abstract and mechanical, but personal, as well—and,
as such, involve not just classifying and categorizing, but continual judging
and feeling also.*
    Oliver Sacks, *The Man Who Mistook His Wife for a Hat*

*The reason you do not clearly understand the time-being is that you think
of time only as passing . . . . Because flowing is a quality of time, moments
of past and present do not overlap or line up side by side.*
    Dōgen, from *moon in a dewdrop*

*Why is it you don't stop suddenly
And retrace your steps
Is memory a feeling that comes at twilight
And when it arrives day's light fades
The seen or the heard wafting by
Like smoke, is contained in a heartbeat
Carried on the breath like a particle*
    Norman Fischer, *I Was Blown Back*

THE SENSUAL INFRASTRUCTURE

Creatures completing ourselves in limbo, partial
Brenda Iijima, *Untimely Death is Driven Beyond the Horizon*

memory
hippocampus cerebellum
amygdala basal ganglia
the song recalls a day

splattered mud by car
the difference of standing
in puddles alongside speeding train
a matter of motor memory

still how the sight
of landscape
harbors time

floral sumbrella
its un-neatly wrapped end

bodies mutually exclusive
but memory?

vehicles in overpopulated city
inharmonious and contingent

phenomenal world
being remains
time

forms inside
without screen
fog across the river
gaps answer
who calls the senses
hell?

small glittering bodies—
fastened
thus plagued

logic
agitation etymology

words unlock barrier or
ferry beyond truth

the most important
if not gravity

no refuge under broken limbs
if not language
then what

sensual infrastructure
a field
sky's mind

senses by way of intellect
mind by way of senses

swimming, or darting,
at the confluence of many creeks

ENCODE

senses first
hundreds of flush blossoms, fragrance,
spring curled around blue sky
hippocampus and frontal cortex analyze sensory inputs
beings bridge distance between bodies and tree—
same speed—still long-term memory-worth
cherry blossoms bloom beyond change
bits stored in brain parts
clap of thunder, water's meander
message leaps and connects across gaps between
nerve cells at synapse
windflowerrain
dendrites, feathery tips of brain cells, extend to neighboring cells
one blossom bears many blossoms
electrical firing releases neurotransmitters
lightning against fence posts
diffuse across spaces between cells
inflorescence snow over earth beneath trees (mind-ground)
as changes occur at synapses and dendrites,
connections materialize
outsidein
first you pay attention
mountains, river, and earth
much is filtered out
thorn bushes
how you pay attention determines what you remember
the old branches, which do not reach

STORAGE

stages served as filters, eschewed overwhelming flood
your favorite color red, as part of (in)eternal palate, a flush color
sensory juncture allowed perception—visual, a sound, a touch
he took the color and engaged any operation
impulses lingered, a moment, after stimulation's end
took the feeling of touch, made it a green room
short term phenomenon breezed in after flash
his figure brushed in orange
repetition and durational shift
"Lady Sings the Blues" is still your song because
you hold the information of him, indefinitely

RETRIEVAL

casting spring   willing unconscious mind
penetrating one thing many   memory elements refining
announcing the stroke   leaving the paintbrush
experiencing the brush   memory of its place
eyes widening   no mismatch   *your grasping*
between cues and encoding
words   letters   *shaping your retrieval*

KEEP

someone is born in a room above a street
a border along dried out river between two states
from seize and hold and observe
dorsolateral frontal cortex arches to air and light

retrieval mediated on right, encoding on left
lace glove, Easter Sunday, braids
words related to looks
maintain—part history, part roots
the fact of being kept, the act of keeping
cortex cholinergic fibers frontal lobe ascend
activate beside seratonergic cords from midbrain
scattered thunderstorms, circuits along sky mind

to take in, receive, contain, hold
to receive with eyes, ears, and mind
to guard, defend, protect, preserve

Purchase to Reading to Fly
(verb and noun coexist)
learning's persistence revealed at later dates
how we place (what we) keep.

THROUGH THE LENS OF MEMORY, TO COLLECT FOR THE NEXT

the distancing of you
somewhat disintegrated, for example
cell (located within)

there are these paper flowers to make for valentine's
(brad through the center of old news)
working the edge

jagged boundaries tie and cut a way to heart center
a blank boat to float
usage and aesthetic

your robe, his coat

our branches
thus

PLACE IS NOT A VESSEL

understanding that home is no-home
listen Aristotle, neither place nor I is a vessel
abandoning home
snowflakes wheel towards ground
this is not measurable as large or small
the backyard tree appears as two legs—V—handstand to the sky.
broaching the subject, it is seven or eight feet
winter so mild, another tree at a distance still with dry amber
leaves unshaken
this is not measurable as near or far
those tiny little flakes today
entering the homeless life
trees aren't moving out there
shivering immediately
look very closely, you see they move barely.
all this is nothing but the way

coordinates

Many memories are, if not expressly about places, richly rooted in them and inseparable from them. Even the idea of "keeping the past in mind" carries with it distinct echoes of location in place, albeit a nonworldly mental "place."
        Edward S. Casey, *Descriptions*

(Looking at something already a memory
(The lines arrive back at themselves.
        Norman Fischer, *I Was Blown Back*

LACUNA

What happened the day the foot slipped, Colorado?

Pay attention. Mind the divide.

Your great-grandmother in the photograph for high school graduation.

*

"We must resort to such stop-gap notions to fill in the rents."

A dozen roses with foliage

placed and remained
                    on her lap.

LONG AGO DREAMING

you knew nothing.
you walked away.
apron's fabric like that five-year-old flowery dress.
you ran through yellow-tendriled sprinkler--
four bathing suit bodies.
Berta's face from below the ironing board.
perhaps I seems an abstraction.
now you are distracted.

how could you know the cost of moving (so often) between the days?

MEMORY OF COMBAT

scientist, scalpel, and seven jars

brain the color of grapes

your arms swing far from low morning light

purplish sky scarred wildly

outsider early, your scrap and tearing,

immigrant orphan

trust the color of memory

cocked or shot

door slam an electrical impulse

so leap or worse explode

mass that arches toward you

aches to erase not memory but

emotion that escorts it

leave hearts for weaker beings

brains, fists: clutches of nightmare

WILD KINGDOM

The invisibility in question can just as well be described as my getting lost in the landscape: as my becoming one with it. Edward S. Casey

crowded around the meat

zebras' entrails to sky

vultures neck deep at the carcass corral

if place drew one inward to this landscape

outward to book: the desert, the dust, the death

who knows the house

or neighborhood

spectacle and fear its own dwelling

this morning a deer tears across neighbor's yard

and not a sound through the window to hear it

PARIS

sometimes a mask no matter how gold pants through pointed nose

bandage spreads by way of skin and forearm
no needle but heroin, and eligible confession

the secreted walls of late-night eighteenth, budget, *jamais vu*
the way memories reside between now and letter after

belied belonging by way of slang
Jardin pleasantries, punk, crush of gravel, a slight rain

outside the addictions, the freckles
combat jacket, chest swells, iced *paroquet*;
boot prints on the bistro floor

MY FUNNY VALENTINE

without thought of that music

derives its haunting power

more by memory than being

by its homogeneity (in other words you're here) so might

you wake this year's red holiday too

I cover the waterfront, I'm watching you

a song haunt certainly its own memorable place

balloons

resist potencies as container

"you can't hate valentine's day"

exerts an active influence on us

Chet Baker, Billie Holiday, and

these words have no idea who you are

TAOS

sometimes a place no matter how lack-lush barks at the mind
under-(re)conceived

gorge expands by way of crevice and anti-shadow
no soul but cocaine, and a hostile

the AIDS floor of the haunted mother-in-law—adobe—a déjà vu
the way memories reside between mind and moving

a piece of paper resisted home in Ashley Pond
(unconsummated & artificial 2AM light)

outside our extinguishing minds, our bodies
carved nickel, spark gauge, the number 6:
metal fragments in an open drawer

INTERPLACE

(freak   *the freak*
I would take back

                             apology carved
                             name's violence

          knelt between oaks
          church parking lot

                                   took / hold
                                   mouth full of him

                             laughter among the key signature

dreaming
—now from interplace   his body
 holds

                    the dreaming
                    body
                    wrenched from fire

          —who paints the mockingbird
        song on the stairs in the middle of the night

fingers laced   unlaced
chest/regret ridges
never stopped loving

                    the suffering   distracted by death's back
                    door lingering   here a hand
                    never thought it would end   like this

                          you were always in two states

(take it back)

in another bird's movement

the disappearing grandfather

of two minds one cannot see the magic
flashing back on all encumbrance

cog in wheel heat the un-enchantment
—birdsong suffocated   on scorched grass

on blue sky   terminated in G—

BELLINGHAM (THE BUTCH SUNRISE MIX)

often a lady, no matter how vicarious the rumors,
dangles at rooftop drunken

tongue explores by way of robe cord and late night
no holds   [bar] tricks between

waterstance and shell

letters language the conduit
abandoned truck and everything girl—untu(r)ned—

come morning   just the view
the bay a mannequin   running shoes draped on a wire

BREATH

mist stuck in lungs, as did the landscape.
breasts barring horizontally, in the old growth above, belong.
forming long-term pair bonds.
one waited to wander the island with such inseparability.
the division of one heart from all others delusion
as the natural tree hollows hold hatched young.
throat's catch. see also the heart leaf spring beauty,
claytonia cordifolia—in the forest understory or streambanks.
candy-shaped flowers materialize on meandering stems.

LETTER TO B

1.

highway therapy

wait for head out window moment (a quiet)...

in fact you in many ways a propeller...

tomorrow we enter the desert field.
not only a geographical space
but a physics field (gold, cacti, chains)—

2.

with fog descending we may no longer see this as home. this country
of old mountains and overtures. the heroine who does not know
her future correlates to the year of endless winter. perhaps false
acquaintances would be overturned with the right kind of traveling.
the weight of betrayal could not be ferried back, so was hung on the
edges of the saguaro where the desert maintained it. fire blossoms.
she finds visions on the west side of the trail. the towns adumbrated,
people unseen.

signs

We revisit places in remembering (just as we do in dreams); and in so doing our minds reach out to touch the things themselves, which are to be found in the very places they inhabit. Mind coadunates with world in memory of place.
      Edward S. Casey, *Descriptions*

Memory is never a precise duplicate of the original . . . .it is a continuing act of creation. Dream images are the product of that creation.
      Rosalind D. Cartwright, *The twenty-four hour mind: the role of sleep and dreaming in our emotional lives*

How much they have to dream about
Because what's out there's lost to them—
They dream in order to place themselves
Back inside their smoking bodies.
      Norman Fischer, *I Was Blown Back*

you're the sister's boyfriend   *you're the sister*

in a bedroom   *bare save the heart-shaped bed*

red satin spread shaped also like a heart   *someone from behind you*

jabs syringe into thigh   *jester figure appears*

podium legs rivet to base   *in brightly colored clothing*

half theater half clown   pointed hat flickers a checkered black and white

the jester faces the scene   in the bed you are the boyfriend who leans in

to kiss the drugged girl   morning you are the girl

who enters the kitchen to find   scattered on all kitchen surfaces

small scraps of paper   with the word "personal"

and the brother who speaks   "everything is personal"

holographic
venomous green
snake with red bands
curls past
your brother
commands be still
each sense a lens
refocusing wave patterns
a context swirls
when lens is moved away
wave interferences
form holographic patterns

synaptic
southern river's shore
sister
snake half coiled
shallow water circuits
despite how still
bites

modular
a cluster of neurons
computes evening water
senses
motor functions
bundles of cat tails
component assemblies
the family gathers

cellular
the snakebite | the leg
hours in the waiting room, poisoned—
no known means by which
tissues other than the brain
are capable of memory storage
but in the morning
your leg aches

spices   lend from   university library

in sandwich bags   spices overflow   tumble out

a handmade art object on exhibit   blends generations of women's

work   the youngest's   (the daughter's)   woven

the grandmother and great grandmother's a dress-length

piece   vintage   geometric   many-colored

when you look at the three generation ensemble   you weep

a tiny car and mini-wheelies to maneuver metal medians.

bridge over the ocean you flip body out window into the sea.

two men stand by ocean's side.

a place to scale extends up below the toll booth.

the men by the railing look on and grin as you climb.

nuclear explosion, people lined up around a park—

square of traffic backed up with motorcycles, babies.

some can see the meltdown happening because they are closer.

news doesn't ripple back.

you are part of a group with access.

with seattle lab technician, you crawl along the ground.

the pulling in
       the taking off
              sounds of a train station
it could rain   *could stretch the track across*
     a thousand bodies
all this time   *to fly from paris to paris?*
      no, the people mutter, toulouse,
never been to toulouse
     you hold a nest or living organism with small thick tunnels
   out of which one bird squirms
       then another more easily flies free

"in laughing class you have to pull it from within" he says handing

you a broken sonnet with a light. "all the world's a stage," you say,

sipping coffee. "laughing is contagious," you add. and the death

goat marched proudly on.

wake with panic open string

first saving a baby monkey

in a neighborhood without the warmth of light

after a boat is flung pitched about at sea

you jump in   sucked into some vortex—

some strong force

deeper you try to swim out

tangled like seaweed

a current or black hole

you make your way to the surface

boat to your left

object to your right

other people swimming

you swing open boat's metal door

carried by ocean gust wind slamming

you leave the door wide

open to the room where the painter

part of the sea scene or no

nuzzles against your neck whispering

"I always loved you,"

his face and body next to you a color myth

there was no day before it was a dream　　*mother and daughter*

unable to live at this age together　　*even for a summer*

evergreen eye movies　　*boxes packed up nowhere to go*

sun settling over peaks　*not long enough for shock at vast changes*

sideways rain running　　*just move the heart*

4pm dark finch songs　　*varying temperaments*

fly back only　　*for the place's radical indifference*

a box with message inside　　*the nightmare lacks presence*

old lover   the married one　　*this body a different back story*

flutter on life's surface　　*rift with ambient breath of its own*

the sun the man the smoke the run　　*bundle of different sensations*

perpetuated flux and movement　　*the sun the man the smoke the run*

even though you can fly you can't make it back and fly across the
building across sand, which extends far beyond the reach of col-
umns. under the bridge beside the sunstruck sea a bird picks up
its kin, nest and all, then rises out of the water, carries the other to
safety beside them. who discusses patterns? you think, if you
lived there you could be at the sea every day. "here my hair so
golden," you wail, but the air's poison. so much unlike the west;
still, you smile as the bird carries its brethren to another home—the
nest gathered around it like wet brambles.

Travis' smell outside the rear window

Lake inside city limits instead of outside

a car swerves then skips

like flat rock over water

bodies left then right

a man loosens doors by way of windows

they sink toward bottom

his hold-the-breath-song

water rushing over him   call this swim

underwater gymnasium a window chorus

two rooms sing space to each other

remorse vertigo at the window's edge

breathe a bit of air

the sound of several legs a syncopated rhythm

displacement of the crash cadence

less a wreck than a careening

music plays behind the two women murmuring above the car's motor

the color of mother-daughter relationship strikes blue-gray a highly intricate book. every page more like a drawer,

a compartment, or a box. you consider how long she must

have saved all the objects that were within every 'page.'

in every 'page' are at least 20 objects—

colorful fish beads, miniature tarot or decorated cards, stones.

every "page" with its enclosed objects contributes to a story.

the objects act as "text(s)," and those texts are a means

of storytelling.

how a poem fits into the day   is it possible to know yesterday

it was more distinct: "raft boats suit your face" a dream walk

along water, reveals plenty of opportunities for my god what you saw

chunks of orange, fragmented geometry. orange and the sea

must already form some picture before you. maybe just a fractured

sun in a way, there at the horizon. even in the dream you thought:

the perfect image. but there was nothing to be remembered not fire as

the sexual object burning over there on the horizon. nothing of the

past at least just the breathless weight of magic. and something

to remember later: undifferentiated, instantaneous, dotlike impact.

isolated objects, spatial points external to each other.

and this morning's wilding difference: the sudden smell of cake.

prouns

*I would suggest that "where have we been?" is often a more
appropriate heuristic device in matters of memory than
"what have we been"?–providing that we do not restrict
interpretation of the "where" to the shrunken sense of site. . ..
Place is the operator of memory, that which puts it to work in
presenting past experience to us in an inclusive and
environing format."*
       Edward S. Casey, *Descriptions*

*Places, even ordinary places, often do much the same:
presenting to us their unreduced verticality over against the
already reduced horizontality of temporal dissolution.*
       Edward S. Casey, *Descriptions*

*If memory is a house well laid out
With foundation stones on bedrock
Then sunlight blazing on the water
Is a stone drilled with tiny perfect holes
full of spatial music.*

. . . .

*The square fields in colors a code
The dividing trees enforcing a code
The only place to be in the words
as if the black lines
Crawling deliberately across the page.*
       Norman Fischer, *I Was Blown Back*

a mansion made of stone binds to self

small fingers coadunate mind and world
clockmaker or cartographer
there is a reason to resist home
over and over windows burst wide open

PROUN

1.

You play in Atlantic waves with a father in limitless space;
his arms, your toes, safety in sand.

Bodies in bathing suits span three dimensions.

The observer, a child, elates the frame.

Helmet cradles head on passing plane. Reverse vertigo averts
sovereign gaze.

Beloved memories conflict what in these spaces, contrail
lines, linear enough to act as ground.

Foundations, a simultaneous tug and shove, movement seen
by angles, sharper lines.

You don't have to understand. What is lost when you ask why.

2.

Mechanism and metaphor constrain one another.

Then they're business proposals.

The woman, windowed, stands at architecture's edge—arch(es)
in the frame.

3.

A penny heads up a message as much as the one heads
down. Languages that aggregate, beyond radicals and with
tones.

Paris, Houston, Portland—events that fold back on themselves.

You understand the continuous surface as multiplication
watching rain bounce off the pavement   envisioning mile-
post as Mobius strip.

PROUN

1.

You've become a product of time's ecstatic proclivity;
you smell the iron.

Father ruffles the hair.

A ground flower made of cloth outside the garden tenders
space.

You lie down in the shroud and see inmates.

Prisons confine whom in the crisis? Arms akimbo, stalwart
enough to act as block.

Cinder the contradiction, rights nuisanced, prominent
figures remain.

You don't have to trail dissolution. What lacks reduction
breathes in this room.

2.

Drone and witness counter one another.

Then they're stone.

A lifetime, geologic, layers terror.

3.

Fabric geometries interrupt the sleeping,

Prayers mutter a stifled injunction.

Letters, rugs, reports—distant but relevant.

You understand mingling shadow with nuance on the wall,

and lower forehead to the sign.

PROUN

1.

For the thousandth time etymology is plunderer. Laughter
chest to groin.

Memory flits across wet pavement, benign morass
of mind.

Morning's dream still mimics Moonlit Sonata. A girl with
bangs redirects the darkness.

A police car skirts the furthest lane—boys young enough
to ease.

Trim and sidewalk, black hair and chain, face bedecked
in shadow.

Thirteenth body surrounded by prescience; the radioman
lacks my calm.

2.

Victim and plunderer serve one another.

Then they're biology.

Fingers blunt instruments of the barbaric.

3.

The smell reaches across the seat.

Power windows reduce the nausea.

Heel taps are my mother; right hand spreads to lilacs.

Left opens the door. Shoulders back, and she doesn't even
hear you coming.

PROUN

1.

You shape the letters to resemble conglomerations
of contours found in natural scenes.

Such characters articulate the landscape.

Look at the root; it says to speak or pronounce. From
whence the Word of God. Identical to bee.

Buzzing above layers in the soil, trees circle, wide enough
to cask the time.

Lumberguts, sheet rock, sap, a building and simultaneous
decay, a lush green.

You don't have to connect dirt to language. But the histories
cave right there.

2.

Memory and soil serve one another.

Then they're the wild frontier.

The posse, gathered—inferotemporal cortex at the encode corral.

3.

Epitaphs point to bodies grabbed by earth.

A caretaker gestures above the grass.

Summer, demolition, cemetery—mortared and undone.

You understand these ants, the frantic movement beyond stillness they cement.

PROUN

1.

You've become a dreamer there, intelligible in terms of
function.

The metal structure beside the train begins the excitation.

Memory traces un-inhibit with continent's crossing.

A rain with luggage check-in settles in the nervous system.

You sift through grammars and find the one.

A flea market borders the periphery, outdoor accents,

difference similar enough in language to comfort.

Street and sidewalk, race ribbons, voices kept at bay.

First morning, plucked from the internal, no urge to speak.

What silence relays.

2.

Potential buyer and salesperson de-sex each other.

Then they're desire.

The stick figure stares at crepe maker as if sure she

embraced him years before.

3.

Dresses for 10 euros line up between the boredom.

Other mornings will prove themselves less divisible.

Rain seeps through tarps; the man wipes away the wet

preoccupations of self.

You get the separation when umbrella turns inside out,

then keep walking without direction.

PROUN

1.

You'd become a woman who had no day before.

A five-year-old Mexican ballet shoe points mood to pink.

Plain grey bricks that house nerves decide the day.

Right or wrong, saucer hovers above the horizon.

Presence flutters why in the meaning(less)—surface details

broad enough to atomize your watch.

Walls, the irony, distance distilled.

You don't have to erase structures of feeling. Place does in

fact provide security.

2.

Body and future exacerbate each other.

Then they're the breakfast table.

You place hands upon the metal, imagine thunderhead

through pines.

3.

A fork shapes the future: Neptune or letter opener?

False fruit aims at absent sky.

Mushroom polymer, biodegradable plate–limitations of now.

You reside near tomorrow.

Gathering air molecules around the skin, you tuck yourself

between years ago and next minute, eye the agitation of an

empty chair.

A fork shapes the future: Neptune or letter opener?

PROUN

1.

You seek a mobile home in him, yet space rises before you;

you linger in the rift.

A patriarch pulls down the truck bed.

House with rock wall beside the lake distracts the beads.

You look through glass and see nothing shorter.

Boundaries contrast what in the ru(i)n, thin delicate lines,

narrow enough to act as string?

House the song, dissonance mitigated, certain things kept
away.

You don't have to bridge the distance. What falls from the
hands.

2.

Chord and boundary might be said to complement one

another.

Then they're Alaska.

The girl, regressed, stands on bow, silences the glacier.

3.

Hurricane remainders blow down makeshift beds.

Cats manifest a disheveled electric.

Tarps, plastic bags, branches—separated but free.

You understand the contradiction by watching wind whip

across the land, then turn your back to the window.

NOTES:

The title "I am another yourself" comes from the Mayan
greeting and code of honor "In Lak'ech," meaning
 "I am another yourself."

Edward S. Casey's chapter from *Descriptions* (State
University of New York Press 1985), edited by Don Indhe
and Hugh J. Silverman, prompted much thought in writing
keep—for "cartography" and "coordinates" especially.

"The Sensual Infrastructure" is in conversation with Brenda
Iijima's *Untimely Death is Driven out Beyond the Horizon*
(a work in progress 1-edition, 2011); *Moon in a Dewdrop:
Writings of Zen Master Dogen*, edited by Kazuaki Tanahashi
(North Point Press 1985); "the song recalls a day" from
Kate Greenstreet's called (Delete Press 2011); "the sensual
infrastructure" from my book Our Parenthetical Ontology
(CustomWords 2008); "Bodies are mutually exclusive" from
Kate Schapira's *operation lifesaver* (edition in four, 2011).

"Through the lens of memory" was written after viewing
Kate Greenstreet's *locating faraway objects* and as a
valentine for Kate and Max.

In "place is not a vessel:" "To study in this manner under-
standing that home is no-home, abandoning home, and
entering the homeless life—this is not measurable as large

or small, near or far. It is beyond beginning or end, beyond
ascending or descending. Broaching the subject, it is seven
or eight feet. Responding immediately, it benefits the self
and others. All this is nothing but the study of the way." The
quote is from Master Dogen's "Body-and-Mind Study of the
Way," Moon in a Dewdrop: Writings of Zen Master Dogen,
edited by Kazuaki Tanahashi (North Point Press 1985).

Contemporary French writer Isabelle Garron's excerpt
from Contemporary Step, translated by Eléna Rivera and in
Aufgabe (Issue 10), was a point of departure for "Interplace."

Some of "signs" was an attempt to render dreams
nonvisually, after reading Oliver Sacks's essay "The Man
who Mistook his Wife for a Hat" in The Man who Mistook
his Wife for a Hat and Other Clinical Tales (Touchstone
1998): "Interestingly, and typically he no longer dreamed
pictorially—the 'message of the dream being conveyed in
nonvisual terms'" (63).

"Panic Open String" is a song by Calexico on Feast of Wire
(Quarterstick 2003).

"Breath" was written for the marriage and pregnancy of
Michael and Adria Magrath.

I discovered El Lissitzky's Proun at the Arthur M. Sackler
Museum at Harvard University in March of 2013. The term

drew me in, making me think at once of prose and noun. Proun is a term El Lissitzky's coined, which he once defined as "the station where one changes from painting to architecture." When I found Lissitzky's definition, I was thrilled to think of the proun relative to memory and place. Though his definition was fairly ambiguous, it possessed a decidedly spatial quality, and the aspect of "translating" from one medium to another interested me greatly. I decided at the museum to write my fourth section of keep as "prouns," wherein I attempted to translate the spatial—the canvas of place(s)—to language on the page.

"Proun (first)" was written after Mei-mei Berssenbrugge's "Permanent Home." For "Proun (seventh)," the following quote from Oliver Sack's *The Mind's Eye*, was key: "Changizi, et al. have found similar topological invariants in a range of natural settings, and this has led them to hypothesize that the shapes of letters 'have been selected to resemble the conglomerations of contours found in natural scenes, thereby tapping into our already-existing object recognition mechanisms.'" (74)

Deborah Poe is the author of the poetry collections *keep (DUSIE)*, *the last will be stone, too* (Stockport Flats), Elements (Stockport Flats), and *Our Parenthetical Ontology* (CustomWords), as well as a novella in verse, *Hélène* (Furniture Press). Her writing has appeared in journals like *Denver Quarterly*, *Bellingham Review*, *Court Green*, *Colorado Review*, *Yellow Field*, *Touch the Donkey*, and *Jacket2*. Her visual works —including video poems and handmade book objects—have been exhibited at Pace University (New York City), Casper College (Wyoming), Center for Book Arts (New York City), University of Arizona Poetry Center (Tucson), University of Pennsylvania Kelly Writers House at Brodsky Gallery (Philadelphia), and ONN/OF "a light festival" (Seattle), as well as online with *Bellingham Review*, *Elective Affinities*, *Peep/Show*, *Trickhouse*, and *The Volta*. She lives in Seattle.